Stay Lit: Turning Scars into Stars and Struggles into Strength

John Roy Capuyon

Published by Obscura Books, 2024.

While every precaution has been taken in the preparation of this book, the publisher assumes no responsibility for errors or omissions, or for damages resulting from the use of the information contained herein.

STAY LIT: TURNING SCARS INTO STARS AND STRUGGLES INTO STRENGTH

First edition. September 1, 2024.

ISBN: 979-8227872739

Written by John Roy Capuyon.

Table of Contents

First off, shoutout to my parents, Jonathan Ang Capuyon and Gina Morales Lapuz. Pops,your strength and hustle taught me how to keep my head up no matter what. Mom, your love andbelief in me kept me grounded when life got wild. I wouldn't be here without you both—madrespect and love.To my siblings, John Paul Capuyon (JP), Jogie Capuyon, and our youngest, John MichaelCapuyon (JM), you've always had my back. JP, Jogie, JM—y'all are my day ones, the oneswho've been with me through the grind. Appreciate you all more than words can say.And to my kids, John Layzie, and my twins, Rayne and Rhian (Kambal), you're thereason I push harder every single day. You give me life, and everything I do is for you. Keepshining, because you're my world.

"Stay Lit: Turning Scars into Stars and Struggles into Strength"

Table of Contents

About the Author

Introduction

"Supreme excellence consists of breaking the enemy's resistance without fighting." — Sun Tzu, *The Art of War*

This book is more than just words on a page. It's a manifesto, a battle cry, and a middle finger to everyone who ever doubted me, disrespected me, or left me for dead. It's for the people who thought I was done when I hit rock bottom, who laughed behind my back, and who counted me out. It's for the ones who didn't think I could do it, who said I needed a team of writers to make this happen, who thought my jail time was the final nail in the coffin of my career. To those who said I wasn't going to bounce back, who assumed my story ended in the cell where I got locked up—I got news for you: this is just the beginning.

This book is for my ex, the mother of my kids, who cheated on me and turned her back when I needed support the most. It's for the so-called friends who disappeared when the shit hit the fan, for the coworkers who looked down on me, and for the people who hated me individually. I hate you too. And this? This right here? This is my payback.

You see, for those of you who don't know how to swallow pills, when this fuckin' book drops and lands in your hands, it's gonna be medicine. And you're gonna take it. Whether you like it or not, you're gonna swallow this truth, even if I have to force-feed it to you. If I gotta put the spoon in your mouth and shove the pill down your throat, so be it. That's what this book is. It's not some feel-good, sugar-coated, self-help bullshit. It's raw, it's real, and it's meant to wake you the fuck up.

"Stay Lit" isn't just a brand I tried to build. It's a philosophy, a way of life. It's about turning scars into stars and struggles into strength. It's about standing tall when the world tries to knock you down, about finding the fire within when everything around you is cold and dark. This book is for the fighters, the survivors, the ones who refuse to stay down. It's for the people who've been overlooked, underestimated, and pushed aside. It's for anyone who's ever been told they weren't good enough, smart enough, or strong enough.

I'm not here to sugarcoat anything or hold your hand. I'm here to give it to you straight, no chaser. My life hasn't been pretty, and I'm not going to pretend it has. I've been a chef, a failed business owner, a convict, and now, just a guy trying to make it in a world that's kicked me around more times than I can count. But you know what? I'm still here. I'm still standing. And if you're reading this, so are you.

This book is about my journey, but it's also about yours. It's about how to keep your fire burning even when the world tries to snuff it out. It's about how to rise from the ashes and come out stronger on the other side. So, if you're ready for some real talk, if you're ready to face your demons and fight your battles, then keep reading. Because this book isn't just for me—it's for anyone who's ever been through the fire and lived to tell the tale.

Let's get one thing straight: I'm not some motivational speaker or self-help guru. I'm just a guy who's been through hell and back, and I'm here to tell you how I did it. This is my story, my truth, and my payback. And when this book reaches you, it's gonna hit hard. So, get ready. Because this is it. This is my fuckin' story, and I'm telling it my way. Stay lit.

Chapter 1: Ignite the Flame - Embracing Your Story

Every story has its rough starts, messy middles, and ends that ain't really ends at all—just pauses before the next shitstorm. This is mine. It ain't pretty, it ain't sweet, but it's real. It starts in Bacoor, Cavite, where I threw down roots for a hustle that would eventually see me through some of my darkest days. But let's not jump ahead just yet.

Back in early 2020, I was clocking hours at Conrad Manila. Five years into the gig, I knew every corner of that place, every face. It wasn't just a job; it felt like a part of my life was wrapped up in those hotel walls. Then, the pandemic hit like a sucker punch. By October, while the world was losing its mind, I was plotting my next move. Out of sheer desperation or maybe some spark of madness, I borrowed a hundred bucks from my mom and launched Stay Lit. It was a simple game—selling high-quality plain tees that no one else in Bacoor was touching. The business caught fire fast because, hell, I was the only game in town.

Things were looking up, right? Well, the universe has a sick sense of humor. Come November, HR at Conrad rings me up, voice colder than a dead man's stare, telling me I'm cut loose. November 30th, marked the end of my five-year stint, and damn, it stung. It didn't matter that I had something else going; losing that job felt like losing a chunk of my identity. But life doesn't let you stop to lick your wounds.

Here's where the story twists. Just when Stay Lit started booming, my personal life took a nosedive. My girl, the mother of my kids, decided to play house with her boss—a married dude from her POGO company. Talk about a low blow. But betrayal wasn't the end of it. Soon enough, every other hustler in Cavite caught wind of my gig and started pumping out their own tees. Competition sprouted like weeds, and my little empire began to crumble.

Now, let me take you way back for a second, give you a slice of history. Think about the old gold rushes. A dude finds gold in a creek somewhere, and before he can stake a claim, every man and his dog are flooding in, pans and hopes in hand, muddying the waters. That's what it felt like. I was that first fool with gold flakes gleaming in my pan, and suddenly the river's swarming with prospectors.

This chapter ain't just about the rise and the fall, though. It's about the grit it takes to stare into the face of a shitstorm and spit right back. Losing my job, the betrayal, the market flooding—it all tore strips off me. But here's the kicker: every strip torn off revealed a layer of me I never knew existed. Tougher, fiercer, rawer.

Embracing your story means owning every fucked-up part of it. It's about knowing that even when you're kicked to the curb, covered in dirt, and left for dead, there's still a spark inside you. My spark started with a hundred bucks and a box of tees. What's yours? Look into the dark corners of your life, the broken dreams, the betrayals. Find that spark. Light it up. Stay Lit.

So, yeah, here I am, telling you all this not because I want your pity or your applause. I'm here because this is about getting real, about showing you that if I can claw my way out of the pit, you can too. This book, this story—it's for anyone who's ever been trampled, beaten, and tossed aside. We're all a bit damaged, a bit broken. But we're still here. Still fighting. Still lighting up the darkness. Welcome to my world—let's get this fire started.

"In the midst of chaos, there is also opportunity." — Sun Tzu, *The Art of War*

Chapter 2: From Ashes to Action - Building Resilience

Resilience isn't just a pretentious term you use to seem smart; it's the real, raw toughness you can only appreciate when you've been knocked down and gotten back up, bloody but unapologetic. The key is to face the challenges head-on and keep moving forward, even when all you want to do is give up. This chapter is about turning suffering into strength and hopelessness into motivation.

Let's slightly rewind the tape. Imagine this: You are in the Wild West in the late 1800s. You're a real, dirt-under-the-fingernails kind of person, not one of those Hollywood types. At a rodeo, you are tossed off your horse and wind up in the audience while dust clouds gather around you. Are you going to lie down? Absolutely not. Before the gathered gasps have subsided, you get to your feet, brush yourself off, and get back on that beast. Resilience is that.

Now, let me take you back to Cavite's streets, where I was attempting to establish Stay Lit as more than simply a brand. I was reeling from Conrad Manila pulling the rug out from under me and my personal life turning into a soap opera. It shakes to lose a career that was your lifeblood, to have your heart broken. What it also does, though, is make you go deep inside to discover what makes you unbreakable.

For me, the first step towards developing resilience was realizing that I had two options every day: give up and die or get up and fight back. I decided to take a stand. It was modest at first. I used to tell myself, "Just get through today," every morning. These days accumulated day by day. I was learning as well as getting by. discovering that my skin become more resilient the more strikes I received.

To put it another way, resilience is similar to developing muscle. Every obstacle and every failure is like a workout in the gym. As you persevere through the difficulty, you gradually gain strength. I became more adept at handling the more crap life threw at me. I didn't give up as rivals swarmed the market, attempting to steal my tees. I used my imagination. I searched for perspectives that they hadn't considered—quantity above quality, customer care over sales pitches.

The unvarnished fact is that admitting that mistakes will be made is a necessary part of developing resilience. You will err, put your trust in the wrong people, and stumble and fall. It's what you do after you fall that counts. Do you acquire knowledge? How do you adjust? Or do you simply continue to make the same errors?

I began to see trends, things that would trip me up. Financial strains and personal betrayals were things I started to expect and brace myself for. It was more important to become intelligent and resistant to nonsense than it was to become cynical.

I have to view every bump as a badge and every scar as a teaching tool in order to develop resilience. It was about turning from a young man who was raw and angry into someone who could absorb a setback and keep going. It was about refusing to let my past—no matter how terrible—dictate my future.

I therefore challenge you to begin where you are. Make use of what you have. Try your best. It is how resilience is developed. It's not about never falling; it's about how fast you get back up, how deftly you turn, and how audaciously you enter the arena again. Recall that the world will continue to deliver blows. You have to choose whether to just lay there and bleed out or to spit blood and swing back. Keep fighting and stay lit.

"The greatest victory is that which requires no battle." — Sun Tzu, *The Art of War*

Chapter 3: The Power of Connections - Navigating Relationships

R elationships are the cash that may either make or break you in the rough and tumble of life's marketplace. In actuality, there are a lot of hustlers in the world that dress like saints, and every handshake could end up stabbing you in the back.

Think back to the era of the Silk Road, a network that crisscrossed the centers of ancient civilizations. In addition to their caravans and merchandise, traders and merchants also depended on the partnerships they created. A convoy robbed and a voyage terminated could result from one misguided companion or dishonest merchant. Reading the man was just as important as reading the map.

This is where the treachery in my story begins. Imagine a former drug dealer who now aspires to be a legitimate businessman. I considered this guy, let's call him Ray, to be a buddy. He made a lot of noise about starting over and being clean. He was a man with street cred and visible scars. He told me he was done with the night runs, and I believed him since we had gone through some tough times together. I supported him and provided him with verified contacts. Together, we were going to emerge respectable and untarnished from the mire.

The truth is that Ray was actually pulling double tricks. I was being set up as the fall person for his nefarious operations while he was moving chess pieces behind the shiny appearance of startup presentations and legitimate company offers. I had no idea that the guy I believed to be my savior was actually putting a noose around my neck.

The snap of the trap was a stark reality-check. It was me, the scapegoat, with a betrayal stench so strong it could suffocate you. Ray? disappeared along with my money and reputation into the haze.

It takes survival instincts to navigate connections in the unfiltered underbelly of a person's personal or professional life. You need to be astute, able to decipher motives and signs like a shrewd prophet. Each new relationship presents a chance for growth and disaster, with one path leading to the other.

Rebuilding meant more than just making new friends after the sting; it meant fortifying my barriers. I began modestly, with a closer-than-ever trust circle. Lesson learned: trust more intelligently, not less. to compare every grin to the magnitude of previous betrayals. must pay attention to both the words and the silences in between. When you're not present, who speaks on your behalf? When the lights go out, who is there for you?

forming the appropriate connections is just as important as forming any connections at all in this chapter of lessons taught through blood. It's about realizing that the people we invite to the table might occasionally be our most dangerous adversaries. It's a discerning game where the object is to separate the glitter from the gold.

Therefore, keep this in mind as you proceed along your path: fortify your relationships with others. Allow those who belong there, barricade those who don't, and watch over the gate at all times. Because the next handshake you have in this life may be the one that gives you a deep cut or one that gives you a lift. Remain observant, prudent, and luminous. Because shadows have nowhere to hide when you light up the proper way.

"He will win who knows when to fight and when not to fight." — Sun Tzu, *The Art of War*

Chapter 4: Breaking the Chains - Overcoming Insecurities

Insecurity is like a shadow waiting to strike, lurking around every corner of your mind when you're at your lowest. It whispers uncertainties, fuels fears, and, if you let it, it will imprison you with more power than steel could.

Step back in time to the dusty streets of ancient Rome, a time when gladiators faced challenges beyond the arena. Every conflict was an internal struggle against their fears and doubts. Imagine walking into the pit and feeling the stares of hundreds of people who are placing bets on your life, knowing that this might be the last day of your existence. The way those men turned their doubt into rage and their fear into fuel is what made them renowned. It was about defeating oneself and the opposition, not just about surviving.

Now that I know, I can go back to the streets, where fights take place in regular lanes instead of arenas. An insecure feeling? I've had enough experience. Imagine a young individual trying to make it in a field where nobody speaks or looks like him, coming from a challenging neighborhood. Every meeting felt like going into that Roman arena, and every pitch like a fight. I heard comments like "I'm too street, too tough, and too illiterate." Hell, at times I was even in their voices.

To address these worries, it wasn't about silencing those voices; rather, it was about changing the conversation. I needed to have the self-assurance to convince myself that I deserved this and that I was worthy of achievement. "I can't" and "they won't let me" had to be swapped out with "I will" and "I'll make them."

I remember suggesting that we stay illuminated in a room full of suits and individuals who probably couldn't find my location on a map even with Google's help. Halfway through, I start to notice the sidelong glances and smirks. My hands shook and my voice cracked. "You're not welcome here," the aging doubt said. However, something gave way after that. I visualized the gladiator from ancient Rome, equipped solely with his unwavering resolve to combat death. I took a straight stance, looked up at the group member who exuded the most confidence, and finished my presentation as though my life depended on it.

I got a discount when I left, which is the nicest part. It was because I had faith in myself, not because they developed faith in me overnight. I learned that day that the most difficult fights we fight are internal ones, fighting against the bands of doubt we bind around our wrists.

It takes consistent work to free oneself from these bonds. It would be beneficial if you addressed every thought that is keeping you back and questioned every worry that keeps you from moving forward. Until the person you see in the mirror is the fighter you want to be, you have to keep walking forward every day.

Your concerns are unavoidable and will never truly go away. But neither will your capacity to overcome them. Every day, you must decide whether to let your worries rule your life or to face them head-on, overcome their restraints, and choose a different route.

Remember that it takes courage to wear your scars as symbols of your success rather than to hide them. Showing yourself and the outer world that what didn't kill you made you stronger is the aim. Never let your brightness be extinguished by the shadow of insecurity. Remain luminous.

"If you know the enemy and know yourself, you need not fear the result of a hundred battles." — Sun Tzu, *The Art of War*

Chapter 5: The Hustle and Heart - Succeeding in Business Against the Odds

Business is more than simply balance sheets and profit margins; it's a never-ending street war in which only the most cunning and resilient hustlers prevail. This chapter is about fighting your way to the top when the cards are stacked against you, not about playing nice.

Let's travel back in time to the rough and tumble California Gold Rush era, when hopefuls and hopeless people delved into the ground as if their life depended on it, and in fact they did. A crafty few stood out among them; they did more than just dig; they also sold the pans, shovels, and hopes of financial success. They observed the hustling behind the forceful appearance and the business behind the gold.

Okay, back to my personal under-the-nails tale. I didn't start Stay Lit with a golden parachute or a silver spoon. It was a hundred bucks borrowed from my mother and a stubbornly dreaming head. In Bacoor, Cavite, I was selling fine simple tees out of my trunk, where no one believed premium could sell. However, they did sell because I wasn't merely marketing a product; rather, I was selling a portion of a dream: the dream of looking stylish and feeling like a boss regardless of your bank account balance.

The fundamental issue is that success creates enemies and jealousy. Not just consumers noticed as Stay Lit began to take off. Rivals appeared like weeds, all vying to match my look or lower my pricing. Not to be forgotten are the traitors who planned to steal my concepts while grinning in my face.

When you're surrounded by sharks, you have to bite harder and swim faster to succeed in business. It entails getting up each day prepared to battle, exert pressure, and hustle. Being the first one awake and the last one to go to bed is key. It's about maintaining an open mind, constantly observing and learning.

There was a rival who attempted to harm my reputation by disseminating false information about my t-shirts being knockoffs. I doubled down when that punch that could have knocked me out came. I set up my products, showcased the attention, effort, and quality that went into each one, and threw a pop-up event. I used that attempt to bury me as a springboard for success.

In the business world, it's not just about what you sell; it's also about how you sell it. It's your story, not simply your goods. People support causes they believe in, and they supported Stay Lit because I battled, sacrificed my life, and believed in it.

Here's the thing, though: the concepts apply equally whether you're mining for gold or grinding in the streets. Recognize your value, identify your niche, and work hard. Never allow obstacles to depress you. Learn from every rejection, setback, and betrayal. Come back stronger, wiser, and more determined by using that information like armor.

Keep in mind that, just as in the streets, the real test of a person's character is not how hard they fall but rather how hard they bounce back. Never, ever forget that the hustle is sold separately. Stay hungry and fired.

"Opportunities multiply as they are seized." — Sun Tzu, *The Art of War*

Chapter 6: Recognize Your Worth - Claiming Your Space in the World

It's not enough to simply realize your value; you also need to demand it and carve it out for yourself in a world that is ready for you to give up. When every door you knock on smashes in your face, it's about asserting your space. You do more than simply exist—you make an assertion, you stand tall.

Go back in time to the craggy 19th-century New York docks, where countless immigrants were clinging with callused hands to hope. Imagine a young Irish man, hardly more than a scrap of a man, who has nothing but dreams in his pockets as he steps off the boat. He doesn't merely become part of America's fabric; rather, he becomes woven into its very fabric, creating a legacy brick by brick by working hard for it every single day and demanding what is rightfully his.

Now fast-forward to my personal battle, which is taking place right now in the midst of this hectic world. When I started Stay Lit, I was selling more than simply t-shirts—each piece represented a piece of me, a tale of struggle and strength. But here's the thing: you have to battle twice as hard to go half as far if you're from the streets, where your hands are more accustomed to heavy hits than handshakes.

Respect is something that must be gained; I discovered this the hard way. I positioned myself at every market and pop-up store, not just as a vendor, but also as a fighter making his imprint. I had others examine me, their eyes following the trail of scars and past transgressions left on my flesh, casting doubt on my abilities and value. What they didn't realize is that every skepticism and scorn I encountered simply made me more determined.

I recall having a conversation at a trade exhibition with a well-dressed snob, and he smirked and told me I didn't belong. Instead of seeing a businessman, he perceived a street rat dressing up. But instead of contracting, I grew. With all of my strength, my voice was solid, and my eyes were flaming with a challenge as I pitched Stay Lit. At the conclusion, he acknowledged that I was more than he had perceived by reaching out a hand in addition to placing an order.

It all starts with that fire, that unwavering faith in your own worth, when you claim your space. It's about creating your own freaking table, not waiting for someone to offer you a seat at the table. It's about understanding that, absent your permission, no one can reduce you.

This is the hard, unvarnished truth: there are a lot of voices in the world that are striving to overpower your own. Keep them from doing so. Talk more, stand straighter, and never allow anyone tell you how valuable you are. Your value is something you define and something you uphold, regardless of where you were raised—on the sidewalks or in penthouses.

Remember, we frequently fight the biggest fights of our lives against our own uncertainties. You conquer the world when you conquer them. Claim your area, be ferocious, and stay light. Because nobody else will do it for you if you don't.

"Appear weak when you are strong, and strong when you are weak."
— Sun Tzu, *The Art of War*

Chapter 7: Dealing with Doubters - Handling Rejection and Criticism

If you're doing anything worthwhile in this life, you will encounter critics and skeptics. They're annoying, unavoidable, and extremely difficult to get rid of—just like the dirt beneath your fingernails. The worst part is that dirt? It's an indication that you're taking initiative, moving forward, and creating something from the ground up.

Let us return to the grim streets of classical Athens, where the most astute minds, such as Socrates, were confronted with the rabble's vitriol. This man dropped truths like bombs, upending the established order and forcing the powerful to examine their own shadows. And how was he paid back by Athens? A cup of poison and condemnation. The problem is that his ideals survived his executioners. He endured their worst, and it strengthened his legacy.

Fast-forward to my personal struggles in the trenches of the boardrooms and the streets. I was certain I would receive criticism when I first started advocating for Stay Lit. People were laughing in my face and telling me that a guy with my experience and record had no chance of creating anything meaningful. I experienced door slamming, orders being canceled, and murmurs going viral.

Here's how I handled it, though: every "no," every giggle, and every hushed word was only more fuel for the flames. I developed the ability to accept criticism and use it as a guide. What do they doubt? What makes me unique? I increased my output and made my tees indisputable. Me being professional? I arrived early, remained late, and made myself unavoidable.

Resilience is key to handling rejection, but introspection is also important. It's all about telling the useful notes from the noise. Certain criticisms, the deep-cutting ones, contain lessons within, harsh, bitter teachings that leave your tongue tasting like blood. You chew them over, take lessons from them, then spew forth the outcomes.

A buyer bluntly informed me once at a big industry fair that my exhibit looked like it was placed up on the corner of the street. Yes, it hurt, but it was the reality. The next time, I made that booth the most opulent place on the floor by pouring every last penny into it. That particular customer? returned with open order book and bright eyes.

In order to deal with doubters, you must recognize that their uncertainty is a reflection of their own limits, not your own. Do they not see what you see? Make it more radiant. Do they hurl stones? Construct a stronghold. All of your detractors and haters are merely unconscious coaches encouraging you to run your race faster.

Recall that while doubters abound, those who rise above them are a rare kind. Choose to be that person. Remain lit as a pledge to yourself, not merely as a catchphrase. Transform their uncertainty into an affirmation. Every stride you take toward greatness is a step closer to it than any rejection, criticism, or sneer. Continue to climb, to fight, and to let them watch you come up.

"He who exercises no forethought but makes light of his opponents is sure to be captured by them." — Sun Tzu, *The Art of War*

Chapter 8: Real Recognize Real - Distinguishing Yourself from the Crowd

The key to succeeding in the hustle of life is to stand true rather than just stand out. Authenticity is the hard reality of remaining true to yourself in a world where everyone else is wearing masks and fake identities. It's not just a fancy buzzword you throw about at networking meetings.

Recall the jazz clubs of Harlem in the 1920s, when icons such as Louis Armstrong played sounds that pierced the hazy atmosphere like veracity. You couldn't pretend to be talented at those clubs with all of the noise and commotion. It was direct, honest, and unvarnished. Armstrong was the music, not just the performer. His genuineness made him a beacon for sincere souls seeking authenticity in an era of performance and imitation.

Let's now bring that feeling into my sphere of everyday existence. It wasn't enough for me to simply throw some designs on t-shirts and call it fashion when I launched Stay Lit. It was about weaving tales of adversity, tenacity, and survival into the fabric. Here's where the rubber meets the road, though: being authentic draws both the real and the false. And the true work is in differentiating between the two.

I discovered early on that not everyone who applauds you is truly doing so. For some, the show is only a means to an end. I noticed faces swarming around when Stay Lit began to gain momentum. Some had smiles that reached their eyes, while others had grins as piercing as knives and secret agendas tucked behind their backs. It took more than just intuition to learn to differentiate between these; it took survival.

Being genuine entails more than just being truthful; it also entails standing out in a society where identities are mass-produced. It's about exuding an aura that is not only sensed but also emulated. I recall showing up at a local fair with my narrative on my lips, my booth set up, and tees on display. Consumers bought into the sincerity of a man who lived up to every word he wrote, not just the clothing.

But there are drawbacks to being authentic. You'll attract jealous people, cynics, and critics. They will attempt to purchase you cheap, sell you out, or water down your truth. This is where you need to be street smarts: recognize your value, your truth, and allow no one, nobody at all, persuade you differently.

Being distinctive doesn't only mean being unique; it also means being who you are all the time. You don't back down when the imposters try to imitate your movements and steal your shine—instead, you double down. Even the skeptics have to take a step back and give you respect since you make your real so incredibly evident.

Keep in mind that being yourself is the best thing you can be in a world where everyone else is too busy being someone else. That's revolution, not just disobedience. Let the fakes catch up; stay real, stay light. Real people can tell real people from fake ones in the end, and the true thing always endures. In this polluted environment, maintain your purity and observe how the true paths open and the true ones come together. That's legacy, not just success.

"All warfare is based on deception." — Sun Tzu, *The Art of War*

Chapter 9: From Convict to Catalyst - Transforming Your Past into Your Power

Life is a harsh teacher who will pound lessons into you until you're either beyond repair or mature enough to see the value in using your wounds as stepping stones. This chapter isn't just about getting by—it's also about using your mess as a teaching opportunity and your test as a chance to shine.

Go back in time to a cat by the name of Saul who lived on the streets of Damascus. This man was well-known for stalking the early Christians like prey, causing them great fear. Then, whoa! Saul's life is turned upside down by a voice from heaven and a brilliant light. He transforms into Paul—the same person with a new purpose—using his prior aggressiveness to preach enthusiasm and mend the things he had previously broken. His guilt turned into strength, and his history into his power.

Get ready for a journey into my personal Damascus. From selling t-shirts to selling, well, let's just say that I wasn't always interested in legitimate business. I learned hustle from the streets, and for a while that hustle wasn't clean. Was apprehended and served time. I know, it's a cliched story. The twist is that incarceration wasn't the end—rather, it was just the darn beginning.

Inside, I had to fight every day to keep from becoming someone I couldn't even look at in the mirror. Inside, I encountered truly hardened cats—lifers who had converted their prisons into classrooms and their punishments into lessons learned lessons. I paid attention and gained knowledge. I was still the same person when I got out, but I was also a man with a plan and a fire that no prison could put out.

All I had when I reentered society was a reputation and a record. But I also saw something. Started Stay Lit as a beacon for people like me who had seen hell and were in need of a light to help them find their way back, rather than just a brand.

Taking ownership of your entire story—the grit, the mistakes, and the dirt—is essential to transforming your history into an asset. It's about reversing the narrative and demonstrating that the streets are where you learnt to fight wisely and for a better cause, just as they taught you how to fight filthy.

I refined the hustler's mentality, keeping the street smarts but adding business acumen. Every "no" and every rejection I received, I used as fuel. I made a badge of honor out of every "ex-con" label they put on my back, proving that anyone could succeed if I could.

The truth is that you are not defined by your past. It makes you more refined. It may be the fire that shapes you into something strong, or it could be a weight that ties you to the bottom. You have a choice.

Therefore, pay attention if you believe that you have gone too far, fallen too much, or messed up too much. This is a warning to wake up. You are not defined by your past. As a launching pad, it is. Make use of it. Take ownership of it. And let them to witness you emerge from the ashes, not only to endure but also to guide, motivate, and forge a path so brilliant that it transforms darkness into daylight.

Remain steadfast and fearless, and never lose sight of the fact that every setback eventually leads to triumph. Turn yours into a legend.

"In war, the way is to avoid what is strong, and strike at what is weak." — Sun Tzu, *The Art of War*

Chapter 10: Stay Lit - Living Your Philosophy Every Day

It takes more than just putting a clever phrase on a t-shirt and calling it a day to live the Stay Lit attitude. It's about living that fire, that unwavering spirit, each and every day, in all you do.

Let's travel back in time to ancient Sparta, where the proverb "Come back with your shield or on it" was a way of life rather than just a catchy movie line. From the time they were able to walk, all Spartans received training in honor, bravery, and unflinching resolve in addition to fighting. Their simple dwellings and the battlefield were both places where they lived out their ideals. It was about a lifetime of unwavering excellence, not the glory of a single war.

TAKE A MOMENT TO RETURN to the streets where Stay Lit originated. This concept was created in the crucible of failures, betrayals, and legal and interpersonal conflicts. It's about choosing to lighten the world every morning even if you know it hasn't given you anything but has instead taken a lot from you.

When you live to stay lit, everything you do is a reflection of that inner fire. It's how you respond to a client, how you handle adversity, how you meet an obstacle. Because the tenet of Stay Lit is to take things on rather than take it easy, it is manifesting even in the midst of aches and pains in every muscle and bone.

I recall beating my chest on the pavement, heart in my throat and tees in hand, each rejection feeling like a kick to the gut. But every night I would add up the sales, but also the lessons learned, the contacts made, the little wins that showed I was still in it and keeping the pressure on.

This is not a lifestyle for the weak of heart. It requires perseverance, guts, and an unwavering heart. When someone says "no," you interpret it as "not yet." You get back up after you fall, if necessary one knee at a time. It's about always striving to improve not only your situation but also oneself.

To be clear, the goal of Stay Lit is to illuminate others' paths, not to blind people with your own brilliance. It's about being a light in the darkness, a guide in the absence of a map. It's about change—mine, yours, and ours. Every t-shirt sold, every handshake, every transaction—all of them contribute to the greater goal of illuminating this world with something genuine, something powerful, something unstoppable.

Here is the conclusion, the last statement, the last line in the sand: Stay Lit embodies more than just a book or a brand. It's a decision for life. It's making the decision to be the warmth on the coldest nights and the light on the darkest days. It's about more than just getting by in life; it's about learning from it, persevering through it, and shining brightly.

Maintain this flame not only for today and tomorrow, but for each and every day you are fortunate enough to breathe. This philosophy, this existence, this fire—all of it is yours. Take ownership of it. Enjoy it. Continue to light. And allow the world to gaze in awe.

"Victorious warriors win first and then go to war, while defeated warriors go to war first and then seek to win." — Sun Tzu, *The Art of War*

Conclusion

As we close the door on our grueling adventure, let's look critically back at the ground we've trodden. This is more than simply a book of chapters; it's a road map of scars and a guide on how to get through life's challenges head-on. "Stay Lit" is an order to stay burning while everyone else is ready to put you out of your misery. It is not a suggestion.

We have experienced fire from the streets to the pages of this book; we have learned to embrace our tough pasts, develop resilience like a muscle, and master the difficult skill of holding true friends close while severing false ones. We've overcome our own fears, made our worst fears into weapons, and hustled our way through commercial conflicts that would make the most ruthless tycoons break a sweat.

CONSIDER THE WARRIORS of antiquity, the ones who depicted history via tactics and blood. They were aware of a crucial fact: all battles, even the ones you lose, teach you something. Like them, we've learned from every setback by transforming suffering into ideas and plans into action.

We've laughed at rejection, spit in the face of uncertainty, and danced on the tombs of our mistakes. In a society that would be all too happy to tell us we are nothing, we have learned to value ourselves. We have demolished the falsehoods, put on our truths as armor, and continued to advance without stopping.

"Stay Lit" is not just a phrase. It's life, lived fiercely and loudly. It's about being the darn storm, not just weathering the storm. Remember this as you turn from the pages of this book to the alleys of your own life: each step you take has the potential to illuminate the darkness and demonstrate that our fire persists through even the darkest night.

So, keep your flame alive. Let it burn in your eyes, in your heart, in every step you take. Be the light that guides, that fights, that ignites. This isn't just a conclusion; it's a commencement. The real hustle starts now. Stay lit, stay fierce, and never forget: we're not just making it through—we're making it new.

Acknowledgements

First off, shoutout to my parents, Jonathan Ang Capuyon and Gina Morales Lapuz. Pops, your strength and hustle taught me how to keep my head up no matter what. Mom, your love and belief in me kept me grounded when life got wild. I wouldn't be here without you both—mad respect and love.

To my siblings, John Paul Capuyon (JP), Jogie Capuyon, and our youngest, John Michael Capuyon (JM), you've always had my back. JP, Jogie, JM—y'all are my day ones, the ones who've been with me through the grind. Appreciate you all more than words can say.

And to my kids, John Layzie, and my twins, Rayne and Rhian (Kambal), you're the reason I push harder every single day. You give me life, and everything I do is for you. Keep shining, because you're my world.

About the Author

John Roy Capuyon is a testament to the enduring spirit of those who rise from the shadows to forge their own path. Born on April 28, 1991, in Angono, Rizal, John's journey is marked by a series of battles fought both in the physical and metaphorical streets of life.

His experiences range from culinary endeavors as a chef in various dynamic environments to the entrepreneurial venture of launching a clothing brand, which, despite its eventual downfall, taught him invaluable lessons about resilience and perseverance. His time behind bars further deepened his resolve and honed his perspective, elements that vigorously inform his writing.

Now working in a BPO, JR utilizes his diverse experiences to connect with a broad spectrum of people, drawing from the deep well of his past to enrich his interactions. His writing is not just a recounting of his life but a beacon for others navigating their own turbulent waters.

In his book, JR adopts the mantra "Stay Lit," advocating for tenacity and unyielded brightness in the face of adversity. He writes not only to tell his story but to empower others, offering his life as a blueprint for overcoming obstacles and embracing one's true potential.

John Roy Capuyon is more than an author; he is a voice for the overlooked, a champion for the underdog, and a real-life example of the power of redemption and the unstoppable force of human will. Through his narrative, he aims to inspire, challenge, and ignite a flame in all who encounter his words.

Don't miss out!

Visit the website below and you can sign up to receive emails whenever John Roy Capuyon publishes a new book. There's no charge and no obligation.

https://books2read.com/r/B-A-XAQGC-ZODYE

BOOKS 2 READ

Connecting independent readers to independent writers.

About the Author

John Roy Capuyon is a testament to the enduring spirit of those who rise from theshadows to forge their own path. Born on April 28, 1991, in Angono, Rizal, John's journey ismarked by a series of battles fought both in the physical and metaphorical streets of life.His experiences range from culinary endeavors as a chef in various dynamicenvironments to the entrepreneurial venture of launching a clothing brand, which, despite itseventual downfall, taught him invaluable lessons about resilience and perseverance. His timebehind bars further deepened his resolve and honed his perspective, elements that vigorouslyinform his writing.Now working in a BPO, JR utilizes his diverse experiences to connect with a broadspectrum of people, drawing from the deep well of his past to enrich his interactions. His writingis not just a recounting of his life but a beacon for others navigating their own turbulent waters.In his book, JR adopts the mantra "Stay Lit," advocating for tenacity and unyieldedbrightness in the face of adversity. He writes not only to tell his story but to empower others,offering his life as a blueprint for overcoming obstacles and embracing one's true potential.John Roy Capuyon is more than an author; he is a voice for the overlooked, a championfor the underdog, and a real-life example of the power of redemption and the unstoppable forceof human will. Through his narrative, he aims to inspire, challenge, and ignite a flame in all whoencounter his words.